RAINFORESTS

Andrew Langley

KINGFISHER
NEW YORK

Kingfisher is an imprint of Macmillan Children's Books, London.

Consultant: David Burnie
Illustrations by Barry Croucher, Gary Hanna, Peter Bull Art Studio

Created for Kingfisher by White-Thomson Publishing Ltd.
www.wtpub.co.uk

First published in 2010 by Kingfisher
First published in paperback in 2013 by Kingfisher

Distributed in the U.S. and Canada by Macmillan, 175 Fifth Ave., New York, NY 10010

Library of Congress Cataloging-in-Publication data has been applied for.

ISBN: 978-0-7534-6938-5

Kingfisher books are available for special promotions and premiums.
For details contact: Special Markets Department, Macmillan,
175 Fifth Avenue, New York, NY 10010.

For more information, please visit www.kingfisherbooks.com

Printed in China
1 3 5 7 9 8 6 4 2
1TR/0912/UTD/WKT/140MA

Note to readers: The website addresses listed in this book are correct at the time of publishing. However, due to the ever-changing nature of the Internet, website addresses and content can change. Websites can contain links that are unsuitable for children. The publisher cannot be held responsible for changes in website addresses or content or for information obtained through third-party websites. We strongly advise that Internet searches be supervised by an adult.

The Publisher would like to thank the following for permission to reproduce their material. Every care has been taken to trace copyright holders. However, if there has been an omission or failure to trace copyright holders, we apologize and will, if informed, endeavor to make corrections in any future edition.
(t = top, b = bottom, c = center, r = right, l = left):

Front cover (leopard) Getty/Taxi; ct Shutterstock/Taras Vyshnya; tr Shutterstock/Harley Couper; br Getty/Tim Flach; tl Shutterstock/Fedor Selivanov; bl Alamy/Steve Bloom; back cover Photolibrary/Morales; pages 4tl FLPA/Kevin Schafer; 4cl Ardea/Thomas Marent; 4tr Shutterstock/Rob Jenner; 4bl FLPA/Michael & Patricia Fogden/Minden; 4br Nature/Shatti & Rozinski; 5tl FLPA/David Hosking; 5r FLPA/Cyril Russo/Minden; 5bl Alamy/Robert Harding; 5cr FLPA/Cyril Russo/Minden; 6l Photolibrary/Nigel Pavitt; 6r Nature/Eric Baccega; 7tc Alamy/Kim Walls; 7r Photolibrary/Geoff Higgins; 7br Shutterstock/Eduardo Rivero; 8 Photolibrary; 9 Shutterstock/Dr. Morley Read; 10 Photolibrary/Nigel Pavitt; 10c Photoshot/NHPA; 10ct FLPA/Gerry Ellis/Minden; 10cr Photolibrary/Les Stocker; 11 Photolibrary/Sgm Sgm; 11tl Shutterstock/Glen Gaffney; 11tr Photolibrary/Werner Layer; 11cr FLPA/Mark Mofiat/Minden; 11c Shutterstock/Lexan; 11cr Photolibrary/Luca Invernizzi Tettoni; 11bc Shutterstock/Elena Schweitzer 12–13 FLPA/Frans Lanting; 12tl Shutterstock/ecoventurestravel; 12bl Nature/Luiz Claudio Marigo; 12br FLPA/Minden; 12c FLPA/Pete Oxford/Minden; 12br Shutterstock/Dr. Morley Read; 13t Nature/Staffan Widstrand; 13b Shutterstock/Nicola Gavin; 14bl FLPA/Pete Oxford/Minden; 14tl Alamy/Imagebroker; 14br Shutterstock/Nicola Gavin; 14–15 Photolibrary/Andoni Canela; 15tr Alamy/Janusz Gniadek; 15bl Photolibrary/Berndy Fischer; 15br Nature/John Downer; 16–17 Alamy/Fabienne Fossez; 16tc Shutterstock/ sdecoret; 16bl Photoshot/NHPA/Daniel Heuclin; 16br Nature/Nick Gordon; 17tr Photolibrary/Ingo Schulz; 17br Nature/Luiz Claudio Marigo; 18–19 Photolibrary/Erwin & Peggy Bauer; 18tr FLPA/Michael & Patricia Fogden/Minden; 18tl FLPA/Michael & Patricia Fogden/Minden; 19tr Ardea/Thomas Marent; 19br FLPA/Minden; 19br Nature/John Waters; 20tl Still Pictures/Montford Thierry/Biosphoto; 20tr FLPA/Thomas Marent/Minden; 20br Alamy/Steve Bloom; 21l Ardea/Thomas Marent; 21r Ardea/Thomas Marent; 22l Nature/Nick Garbutt; 22tr Alamy/Photoshot; 22cr Photoshot/NHPA/ANT; 23cl Alamy/Photoshot; 23cr Alamy/NGS; 23b NHPA/Stephen Dalton; 24c Photolibrary/Morales; 24bl Photoshot/NHPA; 24br Alamy/Gavin Saville; 25bl FLPA/Michael & Patricia Fogden/Minden; 26–27 Photolibrary/Rolf Nussbaumer; 26cr Shutterstock/ClimberJAK; 27r FLPA/Mark Moffett/Minden; 27br FLPA/Tui De Roy/Minden; 28tr Shutterstock/Kletr; 29cr FLPA/Luciano Candisani/Minden; 31tr FLPA/Mark Moffett/Minden; 31bl Nature/Nick Gordon; 32bl Alamy/Arco Images; 32–33 Getty/Stockbyte; 32br FLPA/Hugh Lansdown; 33tl Shutterstock/Shee Shee Klong; 33c Alamy/Ben Oliver; 33bl Alamy/H. Lansdown; 33br Alamy/Danita Delimont; 34bc Alamy/Petra Wegner; 34tr FLPA/Christian Ziegler/Minden; 34cr FLPA/Peter Davey; 34br Corbis/Frans Lanting; 35tl FLPA/Michael & Patricia Fogden/Minden; 35tc Still Pictures/Nicolet Gilles/Biosphoto; 35cr FLPA/Cyril Russo/Minden; 35br Photolibrary/Juniors Bildarchiv; 36 Nature/James Akena; 37tl Photolibrary/ David Kirkland; 37tr Photolibrary/John McDermott; 37c Photolibrary/Loren Mcintyre; 37tr Getty/Grant Faint; 38tl FLPA/Mark Moffett/Minden; 38bl Corbis/Erik de Castro/ Reuters; 38cr Shutterstock/Howard Sandler; 38br Shutterstock/Hvoya; 38b Shutterstock/Hywitt Dywadi; 39tl Nature/Luiz Claudio Marigo; 39tr Alamy/Peter Arnold Inc.; 39b FLPA/Frans Lanting; 40tr Getty/Donald Nausbaum; 40–41 PA/AP; 41tr Photolibrary/Konrad Wothe; 41cl Getty/NGS; 41br Reuters/Parth Sanyal; 43tl Still Pictures/Mark Edwards; 43br Getty/Simon Rawles/Reportage; 48tr Shutterstock/Alexander Chaikin; 48cl Nature/David Noton; 48cr Shutterstock/Howard Sandler; 48bl Nature/Michael Pitts.

CONTENTS

MISTY AND MYSTERIOUS

Inside a rainforest, huge trees tower up into a mass of leaves high above. The leaves block out the sunlight but not the heat. The air is hot and still and very humid because there is heavy rain every day. The misty warmth provides perfect conditions for plants to grow—and these are home to an amazing variety of animals. More species of wildlife live in the rainforest than in any other place on Earth. But this precious habitat is under threat as vast areas are cleared to make way for farmland, roads, and mines.

Canopy

A rainforest has several different layers. At the top is the tangled canopy of leaves and branches. There is more sunlight up here, and the trees grow leaves, fruit, and seeds throughout the year. Most animals live in the canopy because there is plenty of food and few large predators. In fact, many animals never venture down to the forest floor at all.

Understory

Stretching between the lower canopy and the ground is the very damp and hot understory. Only about five percent of sunlight reaches here, so many plants grow bigger leaves to catch whatever light there is. With fewer branches, there is space for insects and birds to fly around. Snakes and lizards move up and down the bare tree trunks.

KEY

1. Quetzal—a bird worshiped as a god by the ancient Aztec people, who lived in Mexico

2. Queen Alexandra's birdwing—the largest butterfly in the world, with wings up to 11 in. (28cm) across

3. Jaguar—hunts for prey in rivers as well as on the forest floor

4. Giant leaf-tailed gecko—has a flat tail shaped like a leaf, and when threatened, it stands up and hisses loudly

5. Mandrill—one of the most colorful of all mammals, with bright blue and red swellings on the face and bottom

6. Rafflesia—produces the world's largest flowers, up to 35 in. (90cm) across, but it smells like rotting meat

Peoples of the rainforest

Small groups of people live in rainforests. They have learned how to survive in this difficult environment. Their bodies are smaller and better at staying cool. Most rainforest dwellers are nomads who move from place to place. They are skilled hunters, and they also gather wild fruit and vegetables.

Forest floor

There is very little light here, and few plants can grow. Leaves and other litter fall from the trees above and cover the ground, where they rot quickly in the humid conditions. Huge numbers of insects live among the leaf litter, including ants and termites. A few large mammals, such as anteaters and jaguars, hunt for food on the forest floor.

5

6

> More than 70 percent of the world's plant and animal species live in rainforests, and many of them are still undiscovered.

THE WORLD'S RAINFORESTS

Most rainforests lie between the tropics of Capricorn and Cancer, on either side of the equator. In them the sun is hottest and rainfall is highest, and the climate varies little throughout the year. These rainforests are known as tropical rainforests, but there is another kind of rainforest in some cooler parts of the world. It is called a temperate rainforest, and it is kept damp not only by rain but also by ocean or mountain fogs.

The American black bear is one of the large mammals that live in the temperate rainforests of Canada and Alaska.

"Nowhere is there more light, warmth, and moisture than in West Africa, Southeast Asia, and South America, from Panama to southern Brazil."

David Attenborough (born 1926)
The Living Planet (1984)

The huge eastern lowland gorilla can be found only in the tropical forests of the Congo in central Africa.

KEY
temperate rainforest
tropical rainforest

EUROPE

Atlantic Ocean

Pacific Ocean

Amazon rainforest

SOUTH AMERICA

Tropic of Capricorn

Rainforest belts

There are three major belts of tropical rainforests across the world. The largest covers the basins of the Amazon and Orinoco rivers in South America. The others are along the Congo River in Africa and from Myanmar (Burma) to New Guinea in Southeast Asia. The biggest temperate rainforest is on the Pacific coast of North America.

> The trees of the world's rainforests produce about 40 percent of the planet's oxygen.

> **EQUATOR**—*an imaginary circle around the middle of Earth, passing in an east to west line*

The Iban people of Sarawak, Malaysia, build wooden longhouses on stilts that keep them high up above river floods.

The estuarine crocodile lives in saltwater areas on the coasts of Southeast Asia and Australia. It is the largest of all crocodiles.

AFRICA

ASIA

Equator

Indian Ocean

Southeast Asia

Tropic of Cancer

Pacific Ocean

AUSTRALIA

THE FALLS OF IGUAZÚ

The giant waterfalls of the Iguazú River on the border of Brazil and Argentina form one of the most spectacular natural sights in the world. The river is fed by heavy rainfall in the surrounding forest. There are 275 separate falls over a horseshoe-shaped cliff stretching more than 1.7 mi. (2.7km). Some of these falls are more than 260 ft. (80m) high. *Iguazú* is a Native American word meaning "great water."

During the rainy season, 20 to 30 times more water falls.

ON THE FLOOR

Where the canopy is thickest, barely any light reaches the rainforest floor. Few plants grow, and in some places the ground is bare except for a thin layer of dead leaves and twigs that have dropped from above. Sometimes a tree falls, leaving a gap in the canopy. Sunlight streams through, and suddenly seeds burst into life. Saplings shoot upward in a race to reach the canopy. The fastest wins, reaches its full height, and soon blocks out the light again.

The tail-less whip scorpion has large pincers for grabbing prey.

The trap-jaw ant has the fastest-shutting jaws of any animal.

Bursting with life

The forest floor provides food and shelter for a huge number of insects. Ants, beetles, and other invertebrates live in the leaf litter or in the soil underneath. These in turn are eaten by spiders, scorpions, and centipedes. Mammals find food here, too. Pigs and rats root around in the litter, while deer eat leaves. They are hunted by other animals, such as snakes and big cats.

> Less than one percent of the sunlight that shines on the top of the canopy makes it down to the forest floor.

> SPORES—microscopic specks that work like seeds, helping simple plants, fungi, and bacteria reproduce

The Goliath bird-eating tarantula is the biggest spider in the world, reaching 12 in. (30cm) across.

Leafcutter ants chew up leaves and grow a special fungus on them for food.

Tongue twister

The African okapi is one of the tallest rainforest animals. Not surprisingly, it is related to the giraffe. It stands almost 6.5 ft. (2m) tall and can reach up to feed on the leaves of understory trees. Its long tongue also helps. The okapi's tongue is so long that the animal can lick its own eyelids.

🌀 FANTASTIC FUNGUS

Fungi are some of the most important inhabitants of the forest floor. They feed on plant tissue and help break down leaf litter. They are mostly invisible, sending out tiny threads under the leaves, but occasionally they send threads up a stem or form structures that come in many shapes and colors. One of the most dramatic structures is the maiden veil fungus, whose tip gives off a disgusting smell.

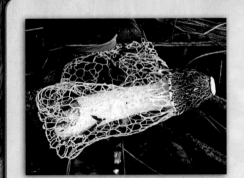

The smell of a maiden veil fungus attracts flies, which spread the fungus's spores.

THE UNDERSTORY

The rainforest understory is a mostly open space stretching from the floor up to a height of about 65 ft. (20m). Very little sunlight reaches this area, and the air is humid, stuffy, and still. A few shrubs and small trees manage to grow here, but the biggest features are the smooth trunks of the giant trees soaring up toward the canopy. Around them is a tangle of vines, lianas, and other climbing plants.

On the up

The understory is home to animals that can fly in the open spaces or climb a short way up into the trees. This includes a huge variety of birds, frogs, butterflies, and other insects. The largest predators, such as leopards and snakes, blend in with the dappled shade of the vegetation as they hunt birds and small mammals.

The Burmese python's strongest sense is smell. It uses its tongue to "sniff" the air for prey.

This python has backward-sloping teeth that grip onto prey while the snake crushes it to death with its body.

Scientists calculate that there may be more than 40,000 species of insects in 2.5 acres (1 hectare) of Amazon rainforest.

> COLONY—*a group of creatures of the same species that live and work together*

10

WEAVING THE LEAVES

In the rainforests of Southeast Asia, colonies of weaver ants make their nests in living leaves. Starting at the tip, they fold over a leaf edge, clasping it with their jaws, and "sew" it to the other side. Their thread is the silky substance produced by the ant larvae (young that have just hatched). The ants work together and use the larvae like tools, gently squeezing them so that they produce the silk that attaches one side of a leaf to another.

These weaver ants are joining two sides of a leaf together.

KEY

1 Burmese python—one of the biggest snakes, at more than 16 ft. (5m) long

2 Tree kangaroo—climbs by holding a branch with its front legs and then hopping with powerful back legs

3 Clouded leopard—so called because its markings look like clouds

4 Flying fox—not a fox at all but a fruit-eating bat

5 Heliconia—a plant related to the banana

6 Rambutan—a tree with fruit that is covered with fleshy spines

Inside its hairy skin, the tasty rambutan fruit is soft and juicy.

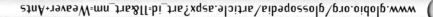

A WORLD IN THE AIR

Imagine you are walking through a tropical rainforest. From the ground, you will see very few animals because most of them live high up in the canopy. The canopy is the roof of the rainforest, perhaps 150 ft. (45m) above the floor, which stretches in an almost unbroken mass of leaves.

The topmost part receives the full strength of the sunlight but shades the areas below. Inside the canopy is a dense network of branches, vines, and hanging plants.

● CANOPY CLIMBERS

Many modern machines can help scientists explore the canopy. People can fly over it in helicopters or balloons, but the simplest and best way is to climb up a rope. The rope's end is shot up into the canopy using a bow, or thrown over a high branch, and tied firmly. People then pull themselves up in a sling using hand grips attached to the rope.

A biologist uses a rope and sling to view the canopy.

The Amazon leaf frog keeps its eggs safe by wrapping them in leaves hanging over a river.

> Tadpoles can live in rainforest trees. Tree frogs lay their spawn in the water that collects in bromeliads and other plants.

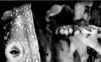

> SPECIES—any group of living things that share common characteristics and can breed together

KEY

1 Canary-winged parakeet—has four toes on each foot (two facing forward and two backward), which help the bird cling to trees

2 Bromeliad—leaves form a "tank" that collects rainwater

3 Red howler monkey—defends its territory by shouting and roaring

4 Three-toed sloth—fur grows toward its spine, allowing rain to run off when hanging upside down

5 Potoo—blotchy plumage and unmoving stance make it look like a tree branch

5

Crowded canopy

More than half of all plant species in the world grow in the rainforest canopy. As well as trees and their fruit, there are orchids, ferns, and bromeliads, which grow in cracks in the trunks and branches. Many animals like to live in the safety of the canopy, where they can find plenty of food. The biggest and noisiest are the monkeys, but there are also beautifully colored birds, reptiles, and countless insects.

4

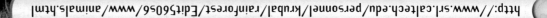

The green monkey of West Africa is actually a light brown color, with a golden-tipped tail. It eats fruit and insects.

OUT IN THE LIGHT

Above the canopy lies a different world from below. The sunlight is dazzlingly bright, and there are often strong winds. Only a few very tall trees poke out above the roof of leaves. These are called emergents, and they can reach more than 33 ft. (10m) higher than the other forest trees. Although they get more light, they also have to suffer higher temperatures, and the wind dries out the moisture in their leaves.

⓵ FRUIT PICKING

Different species of trees often flower and fruit at different times throughout the year, which gives pollinating and fruit-eating animals, such as parrots, a steady supply of food. Parrots are the brightest-colored, noisiest birds in the forest and are some of the best climbers, clinging to branches with strong feet. Many parrots use their beaks to grip higher branches as they climb. Their beaks also crack open nuts and other fruit.

A military macaw eating palm fruit in Ecuador.

Brilliant blue

Morpho butterflies flutter in the shaded layers of forest trees. Morphos have bright blue wings, which make them easy for predators to spot when they emerge in the upper layer. Luckily, morphos are also very fast fliers and difficult to catch.

❯ The leaves of many emergent trees have a waxy coating that helps them lose water more slowly.

❯ **PREDATOR**—an animal that hunts and kills another animal in order to eat it

Living in the treetops

Birds and butterflies can fly easily above the canopy, but for other animals, travel in the emergent layer can be difficult. The branches are thinner, and there is less cover to hide them from predators such as eagles and hawks. There are few treetop mammals, and most are small and light, including shrews, small monkeys, and bats.

Big nose calling

The male proboscis monkey has a long, bulbous nose (proboscis). When the monkey makes its loud honking cry, the nose straightens out. Proboscis monkeys are agile climbers and spend most of their time in emergent trees.

Deadly hunter

The African crowned eagle patrols the sky above the trees. It swoops to catch monkeys and other medium-size mammals with its strong, sharp talons. This eagle builds a large, flat nest in the fork of a tree, just above the canopy.

The sausage tree grows heavy sausage-shaped fruit that can be as long as 3 ft. (1m).

http://www.rainforest-alliance.org/kids/species-profiles/blue-butterfly

JUNGLE GIANTS

More than two-thirds of all rainforest plants are trees. In the colder areas of the world, forests contain relatively few types of trees, but in the perfect growing conditions of rainforests, there is an amazing variety. Scientists have found more than 100 different species of trees within 2.5 acres (1 hectare). There is no winter or summer in the rainforests, so trees lose their leaves and grow new ones at different times throughout the year.

The woolly fibers of the kapok tree are used to fill pillows and mattresses.

Most tree leaves have tiny spouts called drip tips that help drain away rainwater.

Supporting a giant

Many forest trees are about 150 ft. (45m) high, though some grow even higher. The lower half of the trunk is bare, but above this are the huge branches of the crown—the topmost and widest part of the tree. However, these giants have shallow roots, which give little support. If their crowns get too heavy, they may keel over in a storm. To prevent this, some species grow special buttress roots that fan out from the base and prop them up.

Nesting high

The silky marmoset is a small monkey from Brazil that nests in the upper canopy. Marmosets live in family groups of up to 15 and take care of one another's babies.

⊖ TREES ON STILTS

Some rainforests grow on low-lying land, such as coastal areas of Bangladesh, Madagascar, Vietnam, and the Philippines, in the zone between low and high tide. This land is often flooded by the ocean, so the plants that live there have to be able to survive in saltwater. Mangrove trees have developed wide-spreading roots that take vital oxygen from the air instead of the swampy soil. They also act like stilts, supporting the trees and giving them a firm hold in the mud.

Night forager

The agouti searches the forest floor for leaves, buds, fruit, seeds, and even fungi. Agoutis are small rodents, as big as rabbits, that live in South America. Their homes are burrows in the ground, and they come out only at night.

> The tallest tropical tree ever found measured 272 ft. (83m) high. It grew in the rainforest of Sarawak, Malaysia.

CLIMBERS AND STRANGLERS

The trees are the framework of the rainforest, with their huge trunks, branches, and leaves. Many other plants depend on them for support, shelter, and nutrients. The climbers grow up from below. Some of them send out roots that take nourishment from the trees. Others smother their hosts with leaves, depriving them of sunlight and eventually killing them. Smaller plants, such as orchids, ferns, and bromeliads, grow in cracks in the trunks and branches.

A golden-browed chlorophonia nests on a tree covered in epiphytes in Central America.

NUTRIENTS—substances from air, water, and soil that are taken in by plants to help them grow

Flowers without soil

Many flowering plants are epiphytes. This means that they do not have roots in the ground but live on other plants, sometimes high up in the jungle canopy. They get the nutrients they need from decaying leaves that fall onto them from above. Some catch and store rainwater in their cup-shaped leaves, and some of the most beautiful epiphytes are orchids.

Orchid epiphyte

The gongora orchid is an epiphyte with flowers that hang upside down. It produces a dense mass of thin, white roots that spread over the surface of the tree bark. They transport nutrients from dead leaves and animal droppings to the plant.

Pools for frogs

The poison-arrow frog is so called because it produces a poison that some rainforest peoples use to coat their arrows for hunting. This tiny frog is usually brightly colored. Some species raise their young in the pools of water trapped inside bromeliads.

☻ KILLER CLIMBER

The strangler fig begins life as an epiphyte, high up in a tree. As it develops, it sends down long roots to the ground. These carry nutrients and water from the soil up to the fig, which grows quickly. Its leaves cover the treetop, starving it of light. More roots wrap around the trunk, as if they were strangling it. In the end, the tree dies. The strangler fig is now strong enough to stand by itself.

Ropes of the forest

Trees are the framework of the forest, but lianas are the ropes that bind them together. They are everywhere, trailing from the floor to the canopy. Lianas start as small shrubs. They produce long stems, and some have tendrils that grip the tree trunks. In this way, the stems grow upward.

A tree once stood within these strangler fig roots.

> Many people grow jungle climbers, such as the Swiss cheese plant, in their homes.

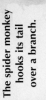

Slim climber

The green vine snake has a thin body and can grow as long as 6.5 ft. (2m). It comes down from the canopy to hunt mice or small birds before climbing back up to rest.

tail grips branch while snake grabs prey

when threatened, large mouth opens wide and head points toward the threat

The spider monkey hooks its tail over a branch.

The fifth limb

Most climbing animals in the canopy have four limbs—two arms and two legs. But some, such as the South American spider monkey, have five. The fifth "limb" is their long tail, which has a movable tip. The spider monkey can bend the tip over and use it as a hook for swinging on branches. The tail is so strong that it can support the monkey's entire weight.

Fast swinger

The orangutan is about 5 ft. (1.5m) tall, but its long arms can span up to 8 ft. (2.4m). With them, it can swing fast between branches. A baby clings to its mother's fur when swinging.

TREETOP TRAVEL

The rainforest canopy is not just a home but a highway for many animals. Monkeys and other primates, as well as snakes, anteaters, and even porcupines, travel easily through the branches. They have adapted so that they can grab and cling to the trees and lianas. Some, like sloths, have claws for grasping tree trunks and move slowly and carefully. Others swing very quickly from branch to branch.

❯ The gibbon (a small ape with no tail) has long arms and can leap across gaps up to 20 ft. (6m) wide.

❯ **ADAPTED**—*changed over time to suit a new environment or situation*

The monkey grasps the branch using only its tail.

long arms reach out to grab another branch

"The extremity of the tail in some American monkeys has been converted into a wonderfully prehensile organ, and serves as a fifth hand."

Charles Darwin (1809–1882)
British naturalist, from his book
On the Origin of Species (1859)

With its hands safe around the branch, the monkey then lets go with its tail and swings forward.

FLIERS AND GLIDERS

Many jungle animals appear mostly at night. Flying creatures patrol the canopy, looking for food. Bats set out to hunt, along with uncountable numbers of nocturnal insects. These, together with moths, owls, and other birds, fly easily in the upper forest layers. But other animals have adapted to this environment. They cannot actually fly up, but they can glide from a high branch to a lower one. Some squirrels, flying lemurs (colugos), lizards, and even frogs grow extra flaps of skin that they use like wings.

Feet that fly

All frogs have webs of skin between their toes to help them swim. But some rainforest species, such as the Wallace's flying frog, use these membranes for gliding as far as 40 ft. (12m). This flying frog lives high up in the jungle canopies of Thailand and Borneo in Southeast Asia. It has extra-long toes, so its membranes are much bigger than ordinary frogs'. It also has flaps of skin on its arms.

Winged cradle

The flying lemur, or colugo, has a membrane that stretches from its shoulders to the tip of its tail. Spreading this out, it can glide for more than 330 ft. (100m). When she is not flying, the female flying lemur uses the membrane as a cradle for her young.

Tail steering

The female sugar glider of Australia glides through the air using membranes between its arms and legs and steering with its tail. She has a pouch on her stomach in which her babies shelter.

> The paradise tree snake is able to glide without a membrane. It spreads out its body by raising its ribs.

> **MEMBRANE**—*a thin layer of skin or tissue between two parts of the body*

"We constantly find details of the marvelous adaptation of animals to their food, their habits, and the localities in which they are found."

Alfred Russel Wallace (1823–1913)
British naturalist and explorer

The frog can change direction by extending or pulling back one of its limbs.

When the flying frog jumps, it stretches out its toes, so the four feet act as wings.

● MONSTER MOTH

The Atlas moth of Southeast Asia has the largest wings of any moth in the world. This huge insect can reach almost 12 in. (30cm) across. The moths lay eggs that hatch into caterpillars. The caterpillars turn into pupae, spinning themselves cocoons made of silk. About four weeks later, they become adult moths and break out of the cocoons. But they live for only two weeks. The moths cannot eat because they have no mouths. They only have time to mate and lay eggs before they die.

adult Atlas moth

HUNTERS AND PREY

Many people think the rainforests are alive with fierce meat-eating animals. Yet there are few large rainforest predators, and they are difficult to spot. Hunters need to stay hidden or their prey will see them. Leopards, jaguars, and other big cats climb trees in search of food or lie in wait in the undergrowth. Other fearsome killers live on the forest floor. Snakes hide in the litter of leaves and twigs, catching rodents, frogs, and even deer.

Top cats

Cats live in the understory of the rainforests. They are some of the biggest and strongest of all jungle animals. Scientists call them "top predators" because they have no natural enemies to fear. The clouded leopard hunts monkeys and squirrels, which it swipes to the ground with its paws. The jaguar ambushes deer and other game animals by leaping unseen from the ground onto their backs.

huge paws and sharp claws used to catch prey

spotted coat mimics the dappled shade of the undergrowth

Death from above

The king vulture lives high up in the canopy. It finds prey by using its sharp sense of smell, swooping on mammals and fish. Like other vultures, the king vulture scavenges on dead creatures using its powerful beak.

◗ KILLERS IN CAMOUFLAGE

Camouflage is a way of deceiving the eye. Different colors or shapes allow animals to blend in with their surroundings so it is hard to see them. This is vital for big cats and other predators that ambush their prey. Leopards and jaguars have dark spots on their fur, and others have stripes. These break up the shape of a cat's body. Smaller creatures, such as insects, also use camouflage to hide from their enemies. Most species of mantis are shaped and colored to look just like leaves.

frock-coated mantis camouflaged on a leaf

> ❯ A full-grown jaguar needs to catch one wild peccary (a piglike animal) each week to stay alive.

> ❯ PREY—animals that are killed and eaten by other animals

large ears pick up the slightest sound

four large canine teeth help grip prey tightly

Poison pump

The bushmaster snake of South America grows to more than 10 ft. (3m) long. It has heat sensors on its head that detect warmth from other animals. Once it has caught the prey in its jaws, the bushmaster injects deadly poison through its fangs.

Hover birds

Hummingbirds, such as this purple-bibbed whitetip from the rainforests of Ecuador, are some of the smallest and most beautifully colored of all birds. Even though hummingbirds are tiny, many flowers are not strong enough to support their weight. The birds hover while they dip their long beaks and tongues down to the bottom of each flower.

long tongue rolls into tubes through which nectar is sucked up from inside the flower

Drinking from flowers

Most rainforest butterflies feed on flowers. Unlike caterpillars (which eat leaves), adult butterflies can consume only liquids, so they drink nectar from flowers. A butterfly pokes its long, thin proboscis into the flower and sucks up the sweet liquid, which gives it energy.

FEEDING ON FLOWERS

Plants, even giant trees, do not last forever. They need to produce seeds, which grow into new plants and take their place. This starts with pollination (the movement of pollen from one part of a plant to another), which creates seeds. Many rainforest plants depend on creatures to help them with this vital process. They attract the animals with food. Hummingbirds, bats, beetles, and bees come to the flowers to feed on pollen or nectar. Their movement spreads the pollen, which fertilizes the flowers.

> Hummingbirds beat their wings up to 100 times every second.

> POLLEN—a fine powder that can create a seed if passed from one flower to another

long, thin, sometimes curved beak is perfect for feeding from long, thin flowers

special joint in the shoulder rotates around so the bird can fly backward

Seed sower

Hornbills have long, curved beaks, with a bony crest on top. They mostly eat insects and fruit, grabbing food in the tip of the beak and tossing it to the back. Hornbills, such as this red-knobbed hornbill from Indonesia, and other birds spread the seeds of fruiting trees, which pass through their bodies and come out in their feces.

⊕ MEAT-EATING PLANTS

Some plants have deadly reasons for attracting animals—they want to eat them. Meat-eating plants have several ways of luring prey. Some have attractive colors, while others smell like nectar. Once attracted, prey is soon trapped. An insect that reaches the bottom of this pitcher plant's deep, jug-shaped leaf cannot escape. The sides either have downward-pointing hairs or are slippery. The insect drowns in the liquid at the bottom and is dissolved and digested by the plant.

pitcher plant attracting an insect

WATER LIFE

Rivers create an extra kind of habitat in the rainforest. For starters, they make large openings in the forest canopy. The trees take advantage of the extra light and form a dense barrier at the river's edge. Water also provides a home for completely different creatures. Specialized plants such as giant water lilies live here, as well as huge numbers of beetles, flies, and other insects. There are also several fearsome river animals, including piranhas and caimans.

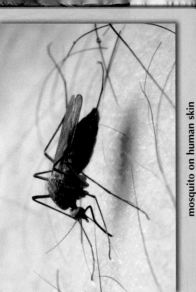

mosquito on human skin

TINY BUT DEADLY

There are many areas of still water in the rainforest, and these places are perfect breeding grounds for mosquitoes, which lay their eggs in water. Female mosquitoes feed by sucking blood from mammals (including humans). When they do this, they may also pick up strains of deadly diseases such as malaria and yellow fever. They will then pass these on to their next victim.

A transparent third eyelid helps a caiman see underwater.

Two rows of sharp, triangular teeth bite off chunks of flesh.

piranha

caiman creeps up on capybara from below

A caiman can grow to more than 13 ft. (4m) long. It lies half hidden in the water and ambushes its prey.

> Native Amazonian peoples use piranha jaws as scissors for cutting wood or even hair.

> **PARASITE**—a small, living plant or animal that feeds on another by living on or inside it

electric eel

Amazon electric eels can produce electric shocks to stun prey or use as a defense.

Rows of special organs on each side of the eel's body release electric charges into the water.

capybara

River grazers

Manatees are large water mammals that can weigh as much as half a ton. They eat mostly plants in shallow water. Manatees spend much of the day sleeping under the water, coming up to the surface to breathe every 20 minutes.

"Pirates, piranhas . . . a lot of mud. It's not polluted water but a lot of parasites were in my body."

Martin Strel (born 1954)
Slovenian long-distance swimmer and the first person ever to swim the length of the Amazon River

Capybaras, the largest rodents, have webbed feet and live in groups of 20 or more.

River visitors

Many kinds of animals are attracted to rivers because they are rich in food as well as water. Land animals come to drink, and swimmers visit to eat water plants or catch fish. Mammals such as capybaras and peccaries make easy meals for a crocodile, caiman, or water snake. The giant anaconda of the Amazon kills by wrapping itself around its prey and strangling it.

JUNGLE PARTNERS

All rainforest animals depend on plants for shelter or food. Even meat eaters rely on plant food because it attracts their plant-eating prey. Many plants also depend on animals to help fertilize them and spread their seeds. Sometimes, animals and plants form special partnerships that are good for both of them. Azteca ants make their homes inside the stems of cecropia trees. In return, they defend the trees against climbing plants and harmful insects.

LARVA—a young animal that looks unlike its parents and that changes shape as it grows older

mealybugs feed on the sap of the plant and produce a sweet juice

ants gather food that the cecropia plant produces

Azteca ants driving off trap-jaw ant by pinning down its feet and feelers

Sap licker

This Maués marmoset is a small South American monkey with clawlike nails and long, narrow teeth. It uses its teeth to gnaw at the bark of some trees. This allows it to lick up the sugary sap or resin that comes out of the wood.

the ant larvae are fed by the adult ants

queen ant chews hole in cecropia stem and creates the first chamber

THE FIG WASP

The flowers of a fig tree grow inside the fruit and are pollinated by fig wasps. Lured by the sweet scent, a female fig wasp pushes her way into the fruit to lay eggs on the flowers. Male wasps hatch and develop first and bore tunnels through the fig wall. After mating with the males, the females escape through these tunnels and fly away. The males have no wings and die inside the fig.

fig wasp starts to push her way into the fruit

Ant tree house

The cecropia is a small tree with a hollow trunk and branches. A queen ant bites her way inside and sets up a colony. She seals herself into the stem and lays eggs, which hatch into larvae and then grow into adult ants that raise the next batch of young. To provide food for the larvae, the ants bring in mealybugs, which give out a sugary liquid that is fed to the larvae. The ants attack other insects that might damage the cecropia and destroy climbing plants that may smother it.

> The biggest fig tree ever discovered in the rainforests had a crown that was 1,970 ft. (600m) in circumference.

FOREST FERTILITY

The rainforest is a very fertile place. The thick mass of trees, shrubs, and climbers grows very quickly. Yet the fertility system is very fragile because the soil of the forest floor is shallow and light. Most of the nutrients are locked up inside the plants themselves. They constantly reuse the same materials, taking in the fertility from rotting leaves and fallen timber before the frequent rainstorms wash it away. The energy of the sun and high moisture levels sustain this cycle of life and death.

"The tropical rainforest is a closed system, with the same nutrients continually recycled. It is so efficient that there is hardly any loss or waste."

Catherine Caulfield
environmental reporter for The New Yorker, from her book In the Rainforest (1987)

● FEEDING ON FOLIAGE

There are no seasons in the rainforest, so tree species shed their leaves at different times. Leaves are the main food of many mammals, but they are made of tough cellulose, which is difficult to digest. Leaf-eating mammals have large stomachs where the cellulose is slowly broken down by digestive juices. Their bodies extract the nutrients and pass out the waste material as dung, which goes back into the soil to feed growing plants.

Chimpanzees usually prefer to eat fruit and insects because leaves are difficult to digest.

KEY

1 As soon as a leaf hits the floor, it starts to turn brown as it decays.

2 Termites chew up leaves and speed their breakdown. They also make nests from chewed-up pieces of wood.

3 A giant earthworm takes leaf fragments into the soil. These worms can grow up to 23 in. (60cm) long.

4 The thin feeding roots of a tree absorb nutrients. Many roots are covered with microscopic fungi that collect nutrients from rotting leaves.

5 A green leaf grows from a young stem out of the fertile soil.

2

❯ New fertility comes to the Amazon all the way from Africa. Sahara sand clouds are blown over the Atlantic Ocean.

❯ **CELLULOSE**—*the tough material that forms the cell walls of plants and wood*

Recycling from roots

Leaves and other debris constantly fall to the forest floor, where they rot and decompose very quickly. This process is helped by the work of molds, fungi, insects such as termites, and many other animals. The rotting releases the nutrients in the foliage back into the soil. These nutrients are soon absorbed by the thick tangle of roots that grow just under the soil's surface. The roots transport the nutrients up into the trees again.

RAINFOREST EVOLUTION

How did rainforests develop, with their astonishing variety of species? Rainforests around the world have a lot in common. They lie close to the equator, have hot, wet climates, and are home to a surprising number of similar creatures. Some are close relatives, but others have evolved the same kind of shape for similar ways of life.

army ants

driver ants

Colony behavior

Army ant colonies, which evolved in Central America, behave in a similar way to driver ants, which evolved in Africa. Both march in columns across the forest floor and do not build nests.

200 million years ago: supercontinents Laurasia and Gondwanaland are still joined

Laurasia

Gondwanaland

170 million years ago: Gondwanaland starts to drift south and break up

North America becomes a separate landmass

Africa separates and breaks away

India breaks away and drifts north

Australia breaks away

Antarctica drifts south

100 million years ago

Regrowth

There are areas where rainforest is regrowing after the landscape has changed. These islands, covered in rainforest, were formed when the Panama Canal opened in 1914.

❶ SEPARATE WORLDS

Southeast Asia was once part of Laurasia, but Australia and New Guinea belonged to Gondwanaland. The two regions developed very different kinds of wildlife. There are monkeys, cats, and deer in the rainforests of Southeast Asia but none in Australia or New Guinea, which have animals—such as the cassowary and the platypus—that are found nowhere else in the world.

cassowary in New Guinea

> There are only three species of lungfish in the world. One lives in Africa, one in South America, and one in Australia.

> **EVOLUTION**—*a process in which living things change slowly over a long time*

Fur versus scales

tamandua

pangolin

The tamandua is a kind of anteater found in South America. In Africa, the pangolin has exactly the same lifestyle, even though it is not related.

KEY

1. Army ants (Panama)—live in colonies that march all together
2. Tamandua (Venezuela)—has thick, bristly fur
3. Black howler monkey (Brazil)—has a prehensile tail
4. Tree pangolin (Cameroon)—has large scales that cover its skin
5. Driver ant (Kenya)—columns can contain more than 50 million insects
6. Long-tailed macaque (Malaysia)—cannot curl its tail around branches

the world today

The main rainforest belts are near the equator

India smashes into Asia, forming the Himalayas

The Malay peninsula and islands of Southeast Asia are formed

Moving continents

About 200 million years ago, the world looked very different. All land was bunched together in two large supercontinents—Laurasia in the north and Gondwanaland in the south. These supercontinents began to drift slowly apart. South America, Africa, and Australia split from Gondwanaland, carrying chunks of rainforest. Over the centuries, most animals and plants on each continent evolved in very different ways, but a few stayed mostly the same.

It's all in the tail

There are species of monkeys in almost every rainforest region. Long-tailed macaques in Malaysia evolved differently from black howler monkeys in South America. Howler monkeys can use their prehensile tails as a fifth limb, but macaques cannot.

black howler monkey

long-tailed macaque

RAINFOREST PEOPLES

Humans have lived in rainforests for thousands of years. They have learned to make the best use of their rich resources. Over the centuries, their bodies have adapted to existing comfortably in the heat and humidity of the jungle climate. Rainforest peoples are able to stay cool because they have little body hair and do not sweat a lot. They are generally smaller than people in colder climates.

Nomadic hunters

The rainforests are difficult places to find food, but rainforest peoples have developed ways to survive. Some are nomads who hunt animals for food. They use bows and arrows to shoot birds and monkeys, or nets and spears to catch larger animals such as deer. Hunters in the Amazon use blowpipes, coating the tips with poison from the poison-arrow frog.

A Ugandan pygmy hunts monkeys— a vital food source.

> It takes about 50 years for a patch of cleared and farmed rainforest to recover its natural state.

> STAPLE FOOD—the major part of a person's diet; usually a starchy food, such as cassava or potato

① FARMING THE FOREST

The rainforests have many wild crops, such as rubber, fruit, and nuts. Rainforest peoples also grow their own supplies of food. They know that the forest soil is poor and thin, so they use a system called shifting cultivation. They clear small areas of jungle, chopping and burning the trees, and plant crops such as cassava, beans, and yams. After two or three years, the soil is exhausted, so the people move somewhere else. The used area recovers and the foliage grows back.

tapping sap from a rubber tree

A village in one house
The Dayak people of Sarawak, Indonesia, live in wooden longhouses. The longhouses are so big that an entire village of a dozen or more families can live together in one building.

Energy giving
Cassava (also called manioc or yuca) is a staple food of the rainforest peoples of South America and Africa. Its starchy roots grow well in poor soils and are a rich source of energy. Cassava is grated and crushed before cooking to get rid of its poisonous juices.

Ceremonial dress
Many jungle peoples, such as this man from Papua New Guinea, decorate their bodies for special ceremonies. Decorations include body paint and large ornaments. They have many purposes, such as showing a person's importance or serving as charms to protect from illness or to bring good harvests.

RAINFOREST RESOURCES

Rainforests are not just wild places full of amazing animals and plants. They are also a treasury of many things that are vital to the planet. Some plants, such as rubber, cocoa, and sugar cane, have become valuable crops worldwide. Many important medicines are produced from jungle plants. Spices, fibers, resins, and dyes come from the rainforest, too. There is also a huge supply of high-quality timber.

Researching the trees

Despite the hard work of scientists, there is still a lot we don't know about rainforests. For instance, how long is the full life cycle of a tree? The tropics do not have separate seasons, so trees do not show annual growth rings.

Inside cocoa tree pods are the seeds from which cocoa powder and chocolate are made.

Colorful crops

Many foods that you see or eat every day come from rainforests. Sugar cane originally came from the forests of New Guinea. Today, it is one of the world's most important crops. Other jungle foods include coffee, cocoa, bananas, oranges, ginger, and peanuts.

Coffee beans come from a tropical plant and are now a major crop in South America and Southeast Asia.

The biggest sugar-cane-producing countries are Brazil and India.

◉ CLIMATE CHANGE

One-fourth of the world's carbon is "locked" in tropical rainforest plants. More than 66,000 sq. mi. (170,000km²) of jungle are destroyed per year, releasing huge amounts of carbon dioxide into the atmosphere. This adds to climate change, increasing natural disasters such as landslides and floods.

flooding and landslides in the Philippines

❯ In the past 50 years, almost one-half of the world's rainforests has been cut down.

❯ **CARBON**—*a substance that (with oxygen) forms the gas carbon dioxide when trees rot or are burned*

Future growth

Scientists can help preserve rainforest plant species that are in danger of extinction. Here, a field worker gathers seeds from the batinga tree, a rare shrub in Brazil. The seeds will be sown so they can produce new trees.

Watching the ground

An Amazon rainforest researcher measures the depth of leaf litter. By monitoring plant growth and decay, scientists can form a better understanding of how rainforest ecosystems work and how the changes in climate affect them.

Many plant species in tropical Kauai, Hawaii, drifted to the island by the ocean and wind or were carried by animals, including people.

The unknown

About half of all animal and plant species live in the rainforests of the world. Every year, several completely new species are discovered, but many are still unknown to us. As the jungle is gradually destroyed, these species may be lost forever. Scientists examine and record the species they find. However, the area covered by the world's rainforests is so huge that much of it is unexplored.

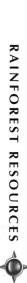

DISAPPEARING WILDERNESS

Tropical rainforests began to disappear many thousands of years ago. Early humans learned to clear land using fire and tools. Over the centuries, the rate of the destruction has grown faster. Today, more people and increasingly large machines are flattening the trees. We are losing a section of forest the size of two football fields every second. Every year, an area the size of Florida is destroyed.

Setting fire to the trees is a rapid way of clearing rainforest

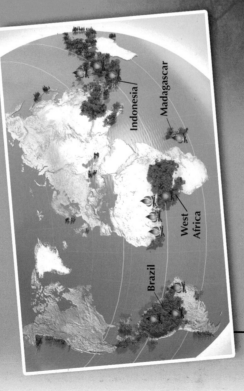

Map of destruction

As this world map shows, some regions of rainforest (marked with flame symbols) have been more badly hit by deforestation than others. Among the worst affected are Brazil and parts of Indonesia, where huge areas are still being destroyed today. More than 70 percent of the rainforest in West Africa has disappeared.

Indonesia

Madagascar

West Africa

Brazil

Smoking ruins

There are many reasons why forests are cut down. Farmers want more land to raise cattle or to grow valuable crops such as rubber and cocoa. Loggers want the timber from the trees to make paper and other goods. As populations grow, towns expand into areas that were once wild. But once the cover of the trees is gone, the soil quickly loses its nutrients. Heavy rains wash out all the nutrients and cause erosion.

> Many famous shoe companies use leather sourced from the cattle farms of the Amazon to make sneakers.

> **DEFORESTATION**—the cutting down and destruction of trees and other growth in a forest

Easy access

Work on the Trans-Amazonian Highway in South America began in the 1970s. This giant road cuts through the rainforest for more than 3,000 mi. (5,000km) from east to west. Other roads cross the jungle from north to south. The highway has opened up the area to even more logging and mining.

Cattle farming accounts for about half of all rainforest clearance. Ranchers "slash and burn" large areas of forest and grow grass for herds of cattle to feed on.

Brutal machines

Logging causes huge damage to the forest. To reach the mature trees, fell them, and remove them, heavy machines destroy the undergrowth and churn up the soil. In many places, the logs are floated down a river to the coast and are then loaded onto ships to be transported to sawmills.

TIGERS IN DANGER

As rainforests shrink and human settlements expand, many animals are losing their homes and hunting grounds. There are probably fewer than 1,500 Bengal tigers alive today. They are being killed by poachers or frightened villagers. This tigress was attacked when it strayed near a village in northeast India. It was rescued by forest workers, taken back into the rainforest, and then released.

tigress leaps back into the wild

THE LAST RAINFORESTS

Centuries ago, there were about 9.6 million sq. mi. (25 million km²) of rainforest around the globe. Today, almost half that vast area is gone—most of it in the past 50 years, due to human activity.

At this rate, the jungles of the world will be completely wiped out by the year 2060. Will the unique plants and animals that live in them disappear as well?

EUROPE

NORTH AMERICA

SOUTH AMERICA

Hunting, war, and habitat loss to farms, logging, and charcoal has made red colobus populations suffer.

slow growth

In some countries, seedlings of rare rainforest trees are planted to reforest areas, but many trees grow very slowly. Mahogany trees can take several hundred years to mature. Mahogany seedlings are shown here.

KEY

1. **Great green macaw (Central America)**—fewer than 2,500 adults remain
2. **Golden lion tamarin (Brazil)**—population has risen from 272 in 1992 to 1,000 today
3. **Red colobus monkey (West Africa)**—population in decline over its whole range
4. **Common chimpanzee (West and Central Africa)**—protected by law in many places
5. **Golden mantella (Madagascar)**—abundant population but in tiny areas
6. **Javan rhinoceros (Indonesia and Vietnam)**—40–60 live in Java and only six in Vietnam
7. **Orangutan (Borneo and Sumatra)**—habitat hit mostly by palm oil plantations
8. **Elegant frog (Australia)**—population lives in only one fragile area of Queensland

Banana plantations, cattle ranching, and logging have deforested much of the great green macaw's habitat.

The golden lion tamarin population, increased by conservation projects, lives in small pockets of recovering forest.

> Well over one-fourth of all medicines used in the U.S. contain ingredients taken from rainforest plants.

> EXTINCT—*no longer existing in a living form; died out*

WORKING WITH THE RAINFOREST

There are ways of preserving the rainforest and harvesting its riches at the same time. One method is to put strict limits on the amount of timber that can be cut down. Another is to learn and make use of the traditional farming methods of the native peoples. Rainforest crops such as coffee, cocoa, and bananas can be grown without needing to clear large areas of forest.

"Destroying rainforest for economic gain is like burning a Renaissance painting to cook a meal."

Edward O. Wilson (born 1929)
American scientist and conservationist

AFRICA

ASIA

felling a tree in Guyana

Chimpanzees suffer from poaching, diseases, and loss of habitat to farms, logging, and oil and gas mining.

The golden mantella's habitat is threatened by logging, farming, settlements, and fires.

Loss of habitat to human interests (farms, roads, mines, settlements, logging, and poaching), plus natural forest fires, has had a bad impact on these once-abundant apes.

The Javan rhinoceros has lost its habitat to farming and through poaching for its horn, which is valued in Asian medicine.

Lost forever

The felling of a rainforest harms much more than the trees. Mammals, birds, insects, and reptiles lose their homes and food sources. Too often, these animals become extinct every year—most of them in rainforests. Estimates show that 9,000 species disappear forever. The destruction also threatens native peoples, who are driven out as the forests are cut down.

Tourism has affected the habitat of this frog, and global warming makes its future uncertain.

GLOSSARY

atmosphere
The layer of gases surrounding a planet.

blowpipe
A long, narrow pipe through which a dart is blown.

bromeliad
A type of rainforest plant from the pineapple family that grows on trees.

buttress root
A projecting growth from a trunk that helps support a giant tree.

camouflage
The shapes and colors that help an animal blend in with its background so that it can hide from its enemies or get close to its prey.

carcass
The dead body of an animal.

cocoon
A covering of silk or similar material spun by the larvae of butterflies and other insects to protect them when they are pupae.

ecosystem
A community of creatures and their environment.

emergent
A tree that emerges (sticks out) above a forest canopy.

epiphyte
A plant that makes its home on another plant.

erosion
The process by which a material is worn away. Soil is eroded by water—especially if there are no plant roots to stop it from being washed away.

evolution
The process of slow change, over many years, that makes living things better at survival.

extinct
When the last of a species has died and there is no longer any of that species living anywhere on Earth.

feces
Dung, or waste matter, from the body.

fertilize
To start the reproductive process in a plant or animal, such as when pollen from a male plant comes into contact with a female plant.

growth ring
The layer of wood produced by a tree in a temperate region, showing one year's growth.

husk
The shell or hard outer covering of a fruit or nut.

invertebrate
An animal that does not have a backbone.

malaria
A deadly, infectious disease transmitted by a mosquito bite.

mammal
An animal with fur that feeds its young on milk.

mature
To be fully grown or developed.

mimic
To copy the behavior or appearance of another animal.

nectar
The sweet liquid produced by plants in order to attract birds and insects.

nocturnal
To be active mostly at night, sleeping during the day.

nomad
A person who has no fixed home and who wanders over a wide area in search of food.

oxygen
A colorless gas in the atmosphere that is necessary for plant and animal survival.

peninsula
A long piece of land that sticks out into the water.

pollination
The movement of pollen from one part of a plant to another, starting the process of fertilization.

predator
An animal that hunts and eats other animals.

prehensile
Describes part of an animal's body, such as a tail, that can hold or wrap around things like an extra limb.

prey
An animal that is hunted for food by other animals.

primate
A member of the group of animals that includes monkeys, apes, and humans.

proboscis
A long, flexible snout. It is also the name given to the long, tubelike mouth of some insects.

pupa (plural: pupae)
The resting, nonfeeding stage during the life cycle of an insect.

reptile
An animal with scaly skin that lays eggs or gives birth to live young.

resin
A liquid produced by a tree that becomes hard, such as amber.

rodent
A mammal with front teeth that grow continually. Rodents use their teeth to gnaw through their food and things in their way, such as plants.

sap
The watery fluid that flows through a tree, carrying nutrients and other essential substances.

scavenger
An animal that feeds on dead remains.

sensor
A body organ that responds to stimuli such as heat, light, sound, or touch.

starch
A type of carbohydrate (energy-giving substance) found in some foods.

temperate
Describes a climate that is neither very hot nor very cold.

INDEX

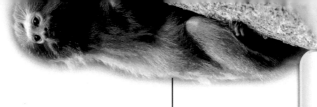

INVESTIGATE

Find out more about rainforests by visiting wildlife parks and tropical gardens or by learning about these amazing habitats in documentaries, movies, and reference books.

Many rainforest species are in danger of extinction in the wild. Animals in zoos are much safer and can be closely studied.

Wildlife parks and zoos

Visit your nearest zoo, where you can get up close to many rainforest animals in captivity, from gibbons and geckos to parakeets and piranhas.

Rainforest by Thomas Marent (DK Publishing)

San Diego Zoo, 2920 Zoo Drive, San Diego, CA 92101

www.sandiegozoo.org

Tropical gardens

See beautiful and extraordinary jungle plants growing in the open air or in special gardens that reproduce the steamy heat of the rainforest.

Tropical gardens, such as the Eden Project in the United Kingdom, preserve many jungle plants and their seeds.

Rainforest Safari by James Parry (Carlton)

Fairchild Tropical Botanic Garden, 10901 Old Cutler Road, Coral Gables, FL 33156

www.edenproject.com and www.fairchildgarden.org

Conservation groups

Rainforests are disappearing fast. You can support or visit the websites of the groups campaigning to preserve these threatened regions, and you will learn a lot, too.

Conservation groups campaign to protect many animals, such as the golden lion tamarin.

Resources and Conservation by Michael Chinery (Crabtree Books)

Rainforest Alliance, 665 Broadway, Suite 500, New York, NY 10012

www.rainforest-alliance.org and www.rainforestconservation.org

Documentaries and movies

If you can't actually travel to the jungle, do the next best thing and watch documentaries or view photographs by wildlife photographers.

Filmmakers record images that give us a vivid picture of life in the rainforest.

Jungles by Frans Lanting (Taschen)

Amazon (Image Entertainment DVD)

http://environment.nationalgeographic.com/environment/habitats/rainforest-profile